THE VERY BEST OF LOVE

nanette newman

CARNIVAL

Carnival
An imprint of the Children's Division
of the Collins Publishing Group
8 Grafton Street, London W1X 3LA

Published by Carnival 1988

Produced by Mander Gooch Callow
Cover illustration by Sarah Forbes

1. God Bless Love © Invalid Children's Aid Association 1972
2. Lots of Love © Bryan Forbes Ltd 1974
3. Vote For Love © Bryan Forbes Ltd 1976
4. All Our Love © Bryan Forbes Ltd 1978
5. The Facts of Love © Bryan Forbes Ltd 1980
6. The Best of Love © Bryan Forbes Ltd 1985

ISBN 0 00 194550 5

Printed and bound in Great Britain by
PURNELL BOOK PRODUCTION LIMITED
A MEMBER OF BPCC plc

Love and Marriage

Mummies and Daddies
and Babies

Friends and Relatives

Animals

The World and Us

GOD...

... in words and pictures

Love and Marriage

2 peepul follin in love xx x

I think you can fall in love if you have your picture taken in frunt of the church.

Eric aged 5

I dont think you know you hav
been happy until   youre not

Mark aged 11

My friend says kissing is worse than haveing flu.

Caroline aged 6

A man fell in love with my auntie on a train but she pulled the cord and he stoped.

Liz aged 6

I shall see how I like being marrid
and if I dont like it I will tr
sumthing else.

Mark aged 11

My sister only wants to get married beause she's a rotten show off.

Peter aged 9

my aunty falls in love
when we go on holiday but
she never likes it and
she cries

Leonard aged 6

I once saw some one fall in love
In a car. It wasn't going though.

Sally aged 7

I Wouldn't fall in love because
girls are all spotty and They
Wisper

Norman aged 6

I think love mean's you
have to buy stamps at
the post office and when
you go to the doctor he
marries you free

Martha aged 6

I know what Love is, its the
stuff they sell on the telly.

Clara aged 4

I've been married five times, mostly with my mother, but once I did get married to a girl who gave me some chewing gum, But that was on holiday.

Leslie aged 7

My big sister fell in love And She went to this place where they Sell you holy matrimony but I Don't think she paid them all the Money because she said it wasn't woth it.

Malcolm aged 7

Love

LO V E

sex is a part of love but not a very good part. Joanna aged 6

My mummy says my Daddy is in love with his car and when I grow up I shall have two.

Roger aged 6

I saw a book once with all drawings on it about falling in love and I think you have to have eggs.

Vera aged 5

Love is hard to do to peeple you don't perticuly like.

Deborah aged 10

Love
it makes you coff a lot

Peter aged 5

my brother got marred   he
didnt fall in love he just
wanted some one older to talk to

Theo aged 7

Why cant you vote for Love?

Brenda aged 8

To get married you have to shave youre legs. I think

Alice aged 5

you have a hart attak if you fall in love to kwickly

Paul aged 7

I dont like to see old ladies
and men getting married becaus
thayre to old for it

Dino aged 6

It is silly to get Married
before you are 12

Edward aged 6

OLd ladys arent reeLy oLd Ladys.
There just pepel waring old
cLothes.

Jamie aged 6

you should never love some one
you dont like much

Katy aged 7

when you marry a girl you have to
give her o best man

Richard aged 6

Mummies and Daddies and Babies

To have a baby you have to make love to someone who doesn't mind

Marianne aged 9

if You put a man and a woman in bed together one of them will have a baby

Paul aged 6

The man next door has a baby in his tummy but it never comes out

Janet aged 6

If you want to have a baby go to the library

Pierre aged 8

I nearly know how to have babies
but we don't do it till next term

Frances aged 7

you can't talk about babies being made
until you are in the 4th form.

Davina aged 10

don t Know how a baby gets there
nd I think Id rather be serprized.

Claire aged 8

it is ggsier to havg a bab if yor a cat

Tricie aged 6

To have a baby the Mother has to lay an egg then the mail cracks it.

Alison aged 8

When you're pregnant you become sicker and fatter and nastier every day

Marianne aged 9

my mother has witish yelleow hare, pinkish eyes and lots of teeth and she is very butifull.

Ann aged 6

When you are a baby your mother feeds you from her bozom but she can only do milk.

Felicity aged 7

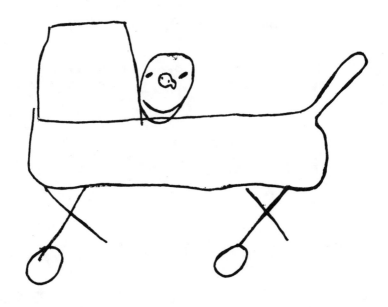

MY   brother   looked horrible
when was born but I didn't say s
because they wouldn't let me
change him.

Leigh aged 6

A baby comes out of the
mummy tummy and bites the Doctor,
and the Docor smacks . it.

Edward aged 6

You should n't have
babies on Sunday because
God wants you to rest.

Merino aged 7

Babies come out of your tummy
on a piece of string.

Graham aged 7

You have to love your own
  baby because everyone else
finds them a newsance.

Patrick aged

BabYs
Dont
grow
On Trees

IF a baby dropz out oF
your tummy When your
zhopping You muzt ring
the police.

Deborah aged 6

You mustn't giv yoew born bady
Sweets its a waste.

Lisa aged 4

Some babies dont want to be born but there
is nothing they can do ab.out it

David aged 6

My father has a cross face in the holedays.

Jean aged 7

my daddy does love me But he Is very Buzy makeing money.

David aged 7

You shoud never help a baby to walk becaus. It falls down and cuts its knee and you always get a smack.

Cormac aged 6

My mummy cried on my first day at school so I had to take her home.

Penny aged 5

Once you've had a baby you can't put it back.

Andrea aged 6

My dad sais he's reading the news but he's only looking at Ladies with no clothes on.

Tim aged 10

my daddy shouts when he speaks a foregn language he doesn't know

David aged 10

My dad likes white people black people chinese people but not people from Tottenham.

Albie aged 7

Peace

My Peace. mummg and daddr like.

They dont often get it.

David aged 7

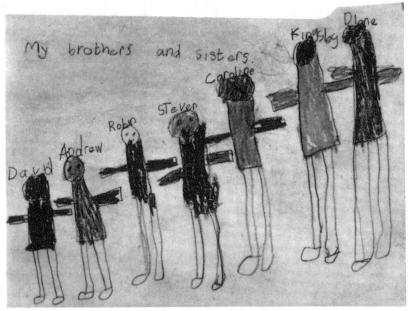

My brothers and sisters.

David Andrew Robn Steven Caroline Kingsly Dlane

My mother said She won't get maried again it's too much truble

Shirley aged 5

When I grow ~~up~~ up I shall have Ilots of babis, Then I'll get married and live happily ever after.

Lisa aged 6

you have to Love your baby brother otherwise ne geos wind

Alice aged 4

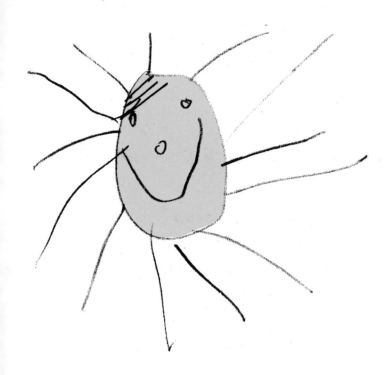

I was adopted so my

parents wanted me

very badly,

Lydia aged 8

Babies are born in hospiral
some mummies bring them home
and some leave them there
for somone else.

Tracy aged 8

Babies are'nt very useful

Brian aged 6

A new borned baby cam't talk it just thinks all day

Tina aged 6

Babies cry in the Dark becorse they thnk they havnt been born yet.

Lorri aged 6

Friends and Relatives

my sister Keeps biting
our Dog

Peter aged 6

FRENDS

I call my friend Whity because
She is black and She calls me
blacky because I am white...
it makes us Laufe

Kate aged 8

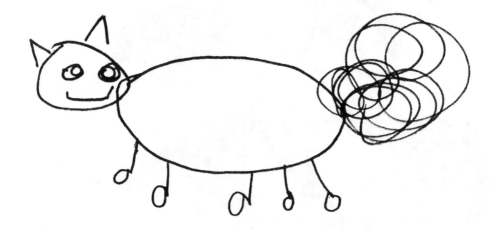

My Granddad says he doesnt
like women So we bought
Him a cat

Robert aged 8

I went to my gran's
funeral to see her elated

Gavin aged 8

I hate spoilt children because they have everything I want.

David aged 8

My friend is Black and I'm pinkish. But we both have the same voice

Diana aged 6

My best friend is gradually becoming a brown person from India

Jane aged 6

My sister and brother tell lyes it runs in the family

Laura aged 8

My big sister has gone To pot and prison

Enid aged

If my sister keeps on
ooking in the mirrer she'll
Turn into a vanity

Susan aged 6

My sister says she eats men
alive but shes only
pretending.

Mandy aged 6

my best enemy is Mark.

David aged 6

Animals

When you know my hedgehog he has a wonderful personality.

Emma aged 10

kittens

My cat falls in love and stays out
all night and then he brings a lot of
kittens back.

Henry aged 6

Guinea Pigs Like
Peace

Emma aged 4

I would like to marry my dog.
but it isint alowed, is it?.

Bruce aged 6

My hamster went to heaven and came back a different colour.

Marilyn aged 6

MY uncle has started to grow to
Look Like a mouse.

Simon aged

Jesus had a cow an

a donkey but I think

he would rather have

had a hamster.

Brent aged

It's sad for cows Because
they're a swear word.

Sam aged

Dear
god.
i hope
you
like my
cat
even.
though
he is
dead
X

I think rabbits make very good mother

Sara aged

My dog wants to give all dogs he meets babies. Nes a terrible responSiblity

Albert aged 7

I had a baby budgie called Tabatha but she died before she knew what she was.

Ruth aged

I bet if animals had votes they'd vote
we didn't eat them

Carole aged 6

LOTS
OF
LOVE
x

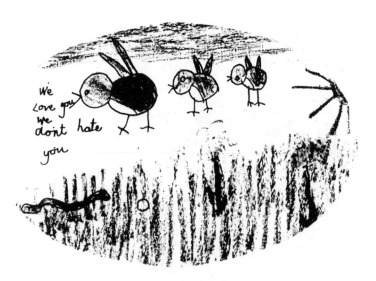

Goldfish are sex mainiaks ~~maniaks~~

Shaun aged 9

I've collected money to save the Prince of whales.

Janet aged 6

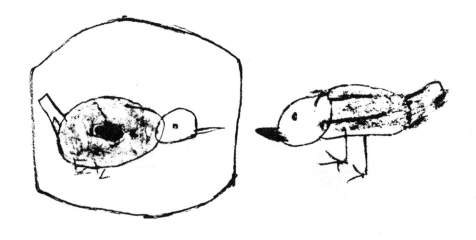

My budgie broke is neck.
It served him rite because
he was always kissing himself
in the mirrer.

Tim aged 6

My dog had lots of babies
When he was young but when
e got old he Jus bit People

Martin aged 7

The World and Us

If a traffic warden sees you kissing in a car you get cramped

Alice aged 6

traffic wardens have to be cross
all day ells they lose there jobb. Tim aged 6

Mrs Thatcher Should do something but I've forgotten what it is

John aged 7

Mrs Thatcher was playing Snakes and Ladders with the queen

Joanna aged 7

On her day off Mrs Thatcher watches herself on tele.

Anne Marie aged 7

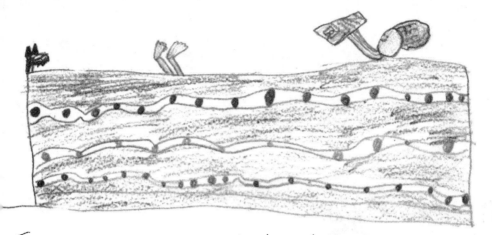

The queen Stays in the bath and does a crossword puzzle on her day off

Richard aged 7

Our Queen does the house work On her day off.

Josh aged 7

They put their helmit on a
chair when they go to bed. Nicholas aged

If they stand in front
of your car you have to
stop.

David aged 6

He leaned right in the car
and my dad said he was drunk.

Scott aged 6

My Teecher is very crule. She smaks Peple all day and she eats frogs legs and maks cros spells. I dont like her becos she says I tell fibs.

David aged 6

I hayt scool and scool lunches and the teecher and all my friends.

Patrick aged 6

Shell

I went to the house of Lords
once, to watch the English play
the Australians

Kevin aged 8

Two Politicians loving each other.

My father says you have to watch out for a prime minister to tell the truth.

Our school cook is a

Secret Poisoner

Sam aged 10

My dad works at being a striker and when I grow up I shall work there as well

George aged 6

A prime minister is so busy he doesn't have time to think

Bruce aged 8

My Friend says my dad is a red but he isn't he's a bus driver

Alex aged 7

I never watch polliticks there
two dangerus

Rhodrey aged 5

When you grow up and get a job
the politicians make you pay
for their taxis.

John aged 8

GOD

God bless my sister
And God bless Mummy And daddy
God bless my toys And friends
And Everyone in the world
And god bless love

Mary had Jesus so that she could get a house.

Christine aged 6

The 3 kings gave Jesus
nasty Christmas presents

Loise aged 6

people like to have
babies for christmas

Anne aged 4

Sun

birds

chrch

I don't think there should be
Rich churches when there
Are poor people

Fiona aged 11

I think Jesus would be
upset if he ~~too~~ knew what
went on at Christmas!

Anthea aged 11

Jesus made his own bread

Pauline aged 6

If I was god I would go to all the countries and say love each other and stop being greedy.

Raj aged 9

I love everybody and everything even ants. god made ants to be loved not trodden on

Ronald aged 7

Jesus wasn't very religuis

Una aged 8

Joseeph's wife Mary had an
immaculate contraption

Cathy aged 7

Jesus was born witha yellow
frill round his head like
his mother

Jeffrey aged 5

My sister is always writing to Jesus an he sends
her chodates an once he sent her Two lots of choclates
on the same day but she won't tell me where to write.

Ian aged 6

I say my Prayers with my eyes open
So I can hear what I um saying.

Robin aged 5

god loves everyone who is good
like me and my friend lucy but
not peopul like gillian who takes
other peoples rubbers

Katy aged 6

Father Christmas and Jesus are best friends

Darryl aged 6

aby Jesus was born with a yeLLow hat on and Kings came to arsk her hand in marage and hey browt her lots of presents. Sarah aged 5

Jesus could have been a pri minister if hed wanted To

Veronica aged 7

Good pepul always friten bad pepul

Mark aged 7

It doesn't matter what you believe in as long as you believe in something

Rosemary aged 12

I think Gods silly because he shoud have painted everybody the same colour and then they wouldnt fight.

Ricardo aged 7

God had lots of children but he ever married which he shood have done

Enid aged 6

This is god